Date: 11/16/11

J 597.872 SOM
Somervill, Barbara A.
Cane toad /

PALM BEACH COUNTY
LIBRARY SYSTEM
3650 Summit Boulevard
West Palm Beach, FL 33406-4198

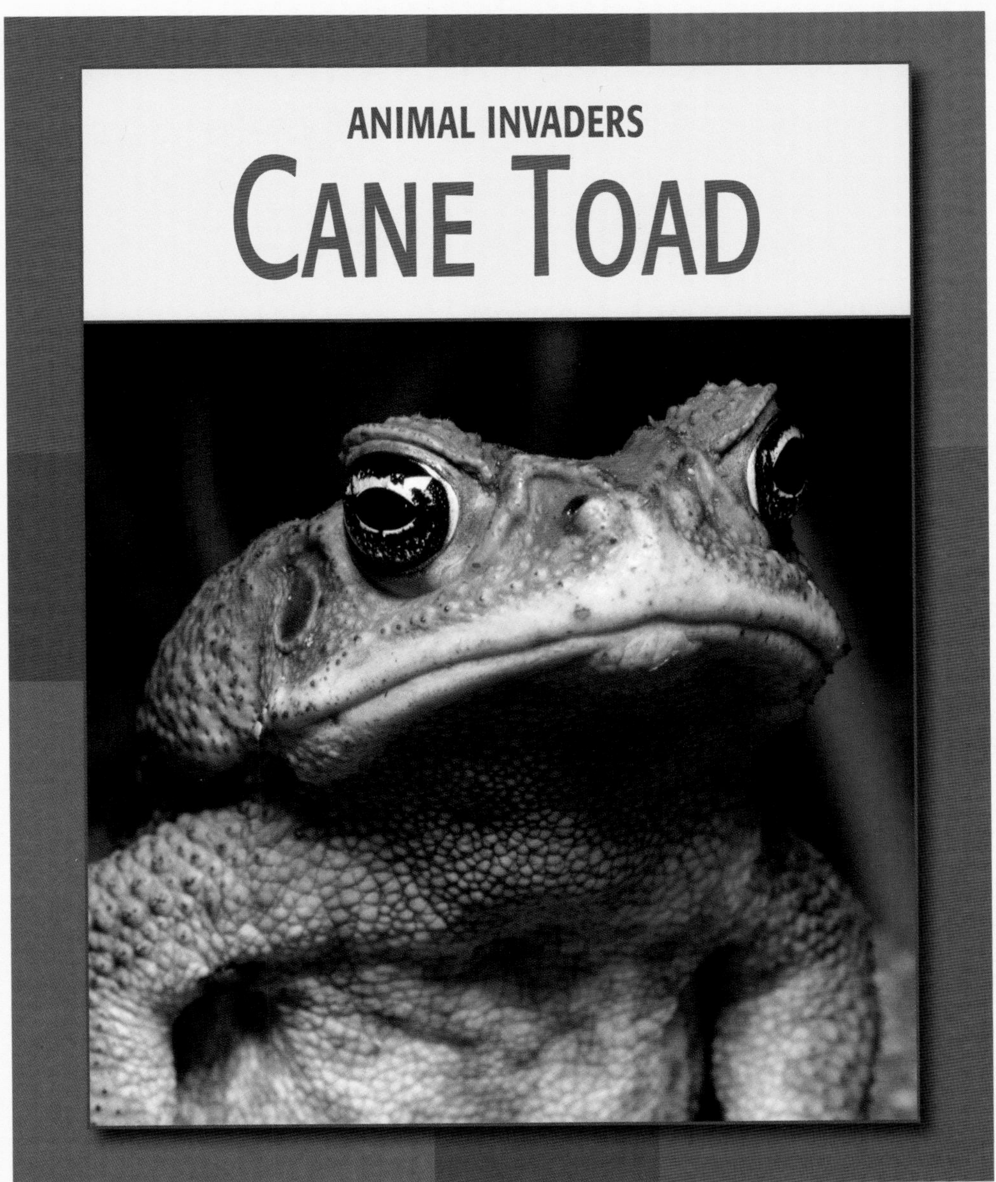

Barbara A. Somervill

Cherry Lake Publishing
Ann Arbor, Michigan

Published in the United States of America by Cherry Lake Publishing
Ann Arbor, MI
www.cherrylakepublishing.com

Content Adviser: Graeme Sawyer, FrogWatch Joint Coordinator, Stop the Toad Foundation Inc., Northern Territory, Australia

Photo Credits: Cover and page 1, © iStockphoto.com/edelmar; page 4, © iStockphoto.com/PaulMorton; page 6, Kevin Enge, Florida Fish and Wildlife Conservation Commission, Bugwood.org; page 7, © iStockphoto.com/ericfoltz; page 9, U.S. Geological Survey Archive, U.S. Geological Survey, Bugwood.org; page 11, © Kathy Atkinson/OSF/Animals Animals; page 12, © W. F. Mantis/OSF/Animals Animals Enterprises; page 14, © iStockphoto.com/PictureInFocus; page 17, © Gordana Sermek, used under license from Shutterstock, Inc.; page 18, © Jack Picone/Alamy; page 20, U.S. Geological Survey Archive, U.S. Geological Survey, Bugwood.org.; page 23, © Danita Delimont/Alamy; page 25, © David Gray/Reuters/Corbis

Map by XNR Productions Inc.

Copyright ©2008 by Cherry Lake Publishing
All rights reserved. No part of this book may be reproduced or utilized in any form or by any means without written permission from the publisher.

Library of Congress Cataloging-in-Publication Data
Somervill, Barbara A.
Cane toad / by Barbara A. Somervill.
p. cm.—(Animal invaders)
Includes index.
ISBN-13: 978-1-60279-115-2
ISBN-10: 1-60279-115-5
1. Bufo marinus. I. Title. II. Series.
QL668.E227S66 2008
597.8'72—dc22 2007033510

Cherry Lake Publishing would like to acknowledge the work of The Partnership for 21st Century Skills. Please visit www.21stcenturyskills.org *for more information.*

Table of Contents

CHAPTER ONE

YIKES! IT'S A CANE TOAD

Johnston's crocodiles, also called freshwater crocodiles, live in northern Australia.

In Lakefield National Park on the northern tip of Queensland, Australia, a ranger comes across a Johnston's crocodile dead on the riverbank. The animal appears to have been healthy. There are no signs of a battle with other crocs—no wounds or damaged limbs.

The ranger is concerned. Was the crocodile infected with a **parasite** or a virus? Could other crocodiles in the area be affected? The ranger carefully wraps the crocodile in a sheet and takes it to park headquarters.

A **veterinarian** is brought in to determine the cause of death. The vet finds the answer quickly. The crocodile ate a large cane toad, and the toad's **toxins** killed it.

It is early evening in a backyard just outside Honolulu, Hawaii. A dog is lying peacefully under a palm tree. Along comes some entertainment—*Bufo marinus*, the cane toad. The dog goes over and nudges it with his nose. The dog decides to play with the toad and picks it up in his mouth.

By the time the owners get home, the dog is in serious trouble. He can't stop drooling and is shaking his head repeatedly. The owners rush to the vet,

Some veterinarians specialize in caring for wild animals. They are called zoological vets, and they work in zoos, wild animal parks, nature preserves, and research centers. These veterinarians play an important role in ensuring the survival of various animal **species**. Dedication, intellectual curiosity, and hands-on experience makes a difference when it comes to protecting the world's wildlife.

Eating a cane toad can mean death for most animals.

but it may already be too late. Their pet bit down on a cane toad, and the toad released toxin into the dog's mouth.

The dog's distress progresses rapidly. His heartbeat has become irregular. The vet washes the dog's mouth out with large amounts of water and administers medicine to control the muscle spasms, drooling, and uneven heartbeat. The dog has arrived just in time, and the vet sternly warns the owners, "Do not allow your dog outside without supervision. Next time, he might not be so lucky."

CHAPTER TWO

All About Cane Toads

The cane toad's natural home includes the Rio Grande Valley in Texas.

The natural range of cane toads reaches from the Rio Grande Valley in Texas all the way down to South America. Cane toads have spread in the rest of the world through intentional introductions and unfortunate accidents. In many places, they are now considered an invasive species.

Invasive species are alien species—animals or plants that aren't native to an area—whose introduction to the area harms the local environment, economy, or human health.

Cane toads have warty skin, bony heads, and ridges above their eyes. Their skin can be gray, yellow, or shades of brown. Their bellies are pale with dark splotches.

As toads go, cane toads are giants. The average adult is about 4 to 6 inches (10 to 15 centimeters) long. Weights vary from 9 to 21 ounces (250 to 600 grams). Adult females are usually larger than the males.

Adult cane toads are active at night during the warmest months of the year. They prefer moist or wet areas. They do not drink water, but they need to soak it up through the skin on their stomachs to survive. A flood can be dangerous for cane toads, as the toads can absorb too much water and die.

During mating season, males attract the females by making a sound similar to a telephone dial tone. This

The skin of a cane toad is warty, and its pale belly has spots.

purring draws females in a frenzy of mating. The males develop special pads on their legs to help them hold on to the females. Females release long strings of eggs, which look like small black beads, that the males **fertilize**.

Cane toads prefer breeding around warm and still or slow-moving water. An adult female can produce eggs once or twice a year. She lays the long, jelly-covered strings of eggs—called a clutch—in the water. A clutch has 8,000 to 35,000 eggs! Only a small percentage of them reach adulthood.

It takes one to three days for the eggs to hatch into tadpoles. Cane toad tadpoles are black with thin, short tails. They are small for tadpoles, measuring about 1 inch (2.5 cm) long. Cane toad tadpoles eat algae or other water plants. Larger tadpoles may eat other toad or frog eggs and insect **larvae**.

Tadpoles reach adulthood in 3 to 20 weeks. Tadpoles take longer to change into **juveniles** when the water is colder and there is less food. It takes juveniles from one to two years to reach adulthood, and cane toads can live for about five years in the wild.

Cane toads will eat almost anything that fits in their mouths. In the wild, they eat beetles, small snakes, other

A cane toad eats a smaller creature.

frogs or toads, honeybees, ants, termites, crickets, small lizards, and snails. Closer to cities, they will eat pet food that has been left outside or even animal waste. Water rats, wolf spiders, crocodiles, crayfish, crows, kites (small hawks), herons, curlews (shorebirds), and snakes prey on

Even the most poisonous creatures can make valuable contributions. In Australia, students in medical schools and biology classes often dissect cane toads to learn about body systems. In addition, research scientists study the toxin produced by cane toads to see if it can be used to help humans.

The cane toad's poison glands give off a milky fluid.

the cane toad. Predators eat cane toads at their own risk.

Cane toads in every stage of life—egg, tadpole, and adult—are poisonous to eat. Cane toads are less poisonous as juveniles than they are as tadpoles or adults. Even so, many creatures die from eating cane toads. Death can occur in many animals within just 15 minutes. The poison acts on the animal's heart, resulting in a kind of cardiac arrest.

Cane toad poison is formed in the **parotid glands**. If bitten or handled roughly, the toad will spray the poison a short distance. Animals that put cane toads in their mouths can become sick or die from the poison. The poison mixes with saliva in the mouth and is then swallowed.

In Australia, quolls (small animals with pouches), monitor lizards, crocodiles, various snakes, and wild dogs called dingoes have died from eating cane toads. Some still had the toads in their mouths when they died.

CHAPTER THREE

Toad Invader

Farmers brought cane toads to sugarcane fields such as this one in Barbados.

How did cane toads become an invasive species? As early as 1844, cane toads were brought to Martinique, Barbados, and Jamaica in an effort to control crop pests. Cane toads were also placed in sugarcane fields in Puerto Rico to get rid of white grubs. While the white-grub population did decline, it's not clear if it was because of the cane toads. However, it earned the toad a reputation as a pest controller.

Suddenly, cane toads were in demand on Pacific and Caribbean islands where sugarcane grew. Scientists in dozens of countries introduced cane toads to get rid of cane beetles, grubs, rats, and other pests for sugarcane growers.

In 1935, scientists shipped 100 cane toads from Hawaii to northern Queensland, Australia. The toads arrived in Gordonvale, where scientists encouraged breeding. If 100 cane toads would help, the logic went, then 3,000

The country with the world's largest population is China. Today, China has about 1.3 billion people. At the rate that cane toads are breeding and expanding, Australia—a country with more than 20 million people—will soon have more cane toads than China has people! What other comparisons can you make that might help people understand the scope of the cane toad problem in Australia?

cane toads would be even better. The cane toads were released into the northern Queensland sugarcane fields.

The main pest for the farmers there was the grayback cane beetle. Unfortunately, this particular beetle travels up the sugarcane stalks, where cane toads can't reach them. Cane toads are large, but they are not great jumpers.

Cane toads have multiplied beyond all expectations in Australia. There are several reasons. First, northern Australia's climate is similar to the cane toad's native habitat in the southern United States, Central America, and South America. Second, Australia's native frogs cannot compete with the larger cane toads. In every way, cane toads beat the competition: in size, numbers produced per breeding, eating habits, and ability to adjust to new habitats. Third, the time period from egg to tadpole to toad is shorter for the cane toads than for any native frog species. So cane toads are producing faster than

Native frogs are much smaller than cane toads.

any native frogs. Finally, Australia lacks successful predators for cane toads.

And so, the 100 original cane toads developed into several thousand; the several thousand into hundreds of

Australia's cane toad population has spread rapidly, covering the northeastern part of the country.

thousands and, finally, into millions. In the northern areas, where the climate is tropical, wet, and welcoming, cane toads have expanded their range by 17 to 31 miles (27 to 50 kilometers) a year.

Experts say that cane toads occupy more than 100 million acres (40 million hectares) of northern Australia. Even if there were only one toad in every affected acre, Australia would now have more than 100 million cane toads. Yet in some areas, there are almost 5,000 toads per acre.

Florida gained its cane toad population by accident. In 1955, cane toads being transported by air had a layover at Miami International Airport. The toads, on their way to a pet shop, escaped from the airport and spread through canals to other areas. Florida has an ideal climate for cane toads, so they thrived. Early in the 1960s, other pet shop owners released another bunch of cane toads. They had no idea that the cane toads would create such problems.

CHAPTER FOUR

Problems and More Problems

Cane toads now live on several continents.

Today, cane toads have invaded more than 50 countries. They can be found in North America, South America, Australia, and Asia as well as on many islands in the Pacific Ocean. The cane toad problem in Australia is far worse than in any other nation, however.

In Hawaii, more than 50 dogs each year die from cane toad poisoning. In rare cases, toads make cats sick or cause them to die. Swallowing even small amounts of the poison can endanger animals. Wherever cane toads are present, some native animal populations suffer, too.

Humans have died from eating adult toads or soups or stews made from cane toad eggs. The toxin can be far more serious for children than adults. Children have smaller bodies that are quickly affected by the poison. Toxin in the eyes causes severe pain. Thorough washing with water cleans the poison from eyes.

Herpetologists are scientists who study **reptiles** and **amphibians**. That includes snakes, frogs, toads, and lizards. These scientists work in museums, zoos, research centers, and universities. Herpetologists have collected the **venom** of various species to make a cure for snake and other bites, called antivenom. Venom from reptiles and amphibians may also be used to control conditions such as diabetes, heart disease, and nervous disorders. Scientists working together and building on previous knowledge are making the world a safer place. Collaboration skills are important to success in almost every field.

Harvard University biologist Edward O. Wilson has said that introducing alien species into a habitat is the second-leading cause of animals and plants dying out. (Habitat loss is the leading cause.)

This is what happened to the dodo bird, a flightless bird found only on the Mauritius Islands in the Indian Ocean. As foreign ships arrived in Mauritius, so did dogs, pigs, cats, rats, and short-tailed monkeys called macaques. These alien animal species killed dodos and raided eggs from dodo nests. The alien species survived; the dodo did not. Do you think cane toads cause a similar problem in Australia, Hawaii, or the Caribbean? Do you agree with Professor Wilson?

In some cultures, cane toad poison is considered a medicine. In Japan, the poison is supposed to restore hair loss in bald men. Some Chinese doctors are considering using the toxin to reduce patients' heart rates during heart surgery.

There is also a growing problem with teens licking the skin of cane toads. Teenagers believe that a small quantity of the toxin can have the same effect as some illegal drugs. This activity is extremely dangerous and can be deadly.

Herpetologists are concerned that cane toads may do better in their new environment than native frogs.

The two groups feed on the same foods, breed in the same locations, and rely on ponds for their breeding. The cane toad produces far more eggs and tadpoles than native species. Tadpoles eat nearly all the same foods, so the first ones to hatch have a major advantage. They eat their fill of available foods, including the eggs of native frogs. And as adults, cane toads eat more different types of food than native frogs and other small creatures, which is another advantage. Scientists are not sure how much of an impact cane toads have on

Like native frogs, cane toads need a water source to live and to breed.

other species that live in the same habitat and feed on the same foods.

Interestingly, cane toads are not a serious problem in their native lands. Cane toads in the Americas are part of the normal ecosystem. There are natural predators that hunt the cane toads. In Australia, however, there are not enough natural predators, natural diseases, or parasites to reduce the cane toad population.

The range of cane toads is constantly expanding in Australia, in part from toads hitchhiking. That's right! The toads may travel on trucks carrying logs to lumber mills or even in passenger cars. As long as there is water along the route, the toads will continue to expand, searching for new breeding and feeding grounds.

CHAPTER FIVE

SOLUTIONS IN THE WORKS

A cane toad sits inside a plastic bag south of Darwin, Australia, after FrogWatch founder Graeme Sawyer removed it from his trap. Traps help reduce the spread of cane toads in Australia.

There is no question that the cane toads in Australia must go. How the country can rid itself of the unwanted amphibians is not quite as clear. The problem is so large that several different methods of control are necessary for success. These methods might be physical or **biological**.

Physical methods of toad control include fencing in ponds and slow-moving streams where toads are likely to lay their eggs. Unfortunately, the fencing also keeps out other animals that need to drink from the pond. Toad traps and toad collections reduce the number of toads in an area but cannot get rid of the problem. Collecting and destroying eggs and tadpoles is the best, cheapest way to curb the population. However, those who do the collecting must be sure they have found the eggs and tadpoles of cane toads, not native frogs.

Biological controls include predators, prey, viruses, and toxins. In places without sufficient natural predators, introducing new predators is not really an option. Introducing new alien species simply reproduces the problem created by bringing in cane toads. Scientists, for example, have discovered that the lavender beetle attracts cane toads and then poisons the toads when eaten.

However, producing enough lavender beetles to destroy the cane toads would create a new problem—too many lavender beetles!

Viruses and toxins present similar challenges. The viruses might affect other species, or the cane toads may be able to survive the illness. Toxins are never a good answer. It is impossible to find a poison that affects only one species with no negative side effects on others.

The cane toad problem arose because planners did not know enough about cane toads and their life cycles. All the suggested solutions require careful study, so that they don't create new, equally severe problems.

In Australia's Northern Territory, ordinary citizens have become the last line of defense against the onslaught of cane toads. Many have joined a group called FrogWatch, founded by teacher and computer whiz Graeme Sawyer. Volunteers set traps in their backyards, fence in ponds that might attract cane toads, and take part in ToadBusts. At ToadBusts, people collect adult toads and remove strings of eggs and tadpoles from standing and slow-moving water in the area. Can you think of any other ways to prevent the advance of cane toads into an area?

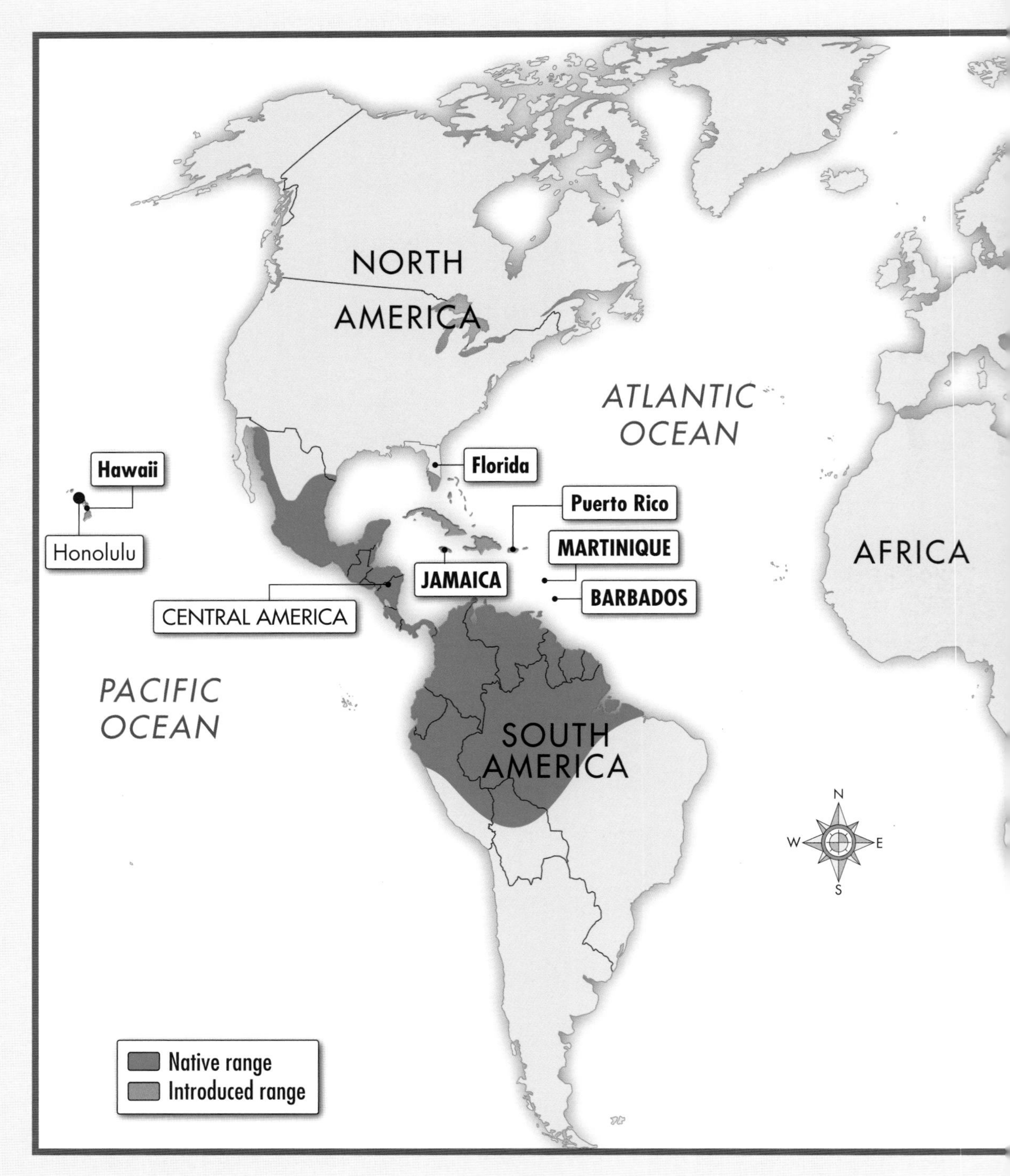

This map shows where in the world the cane toad

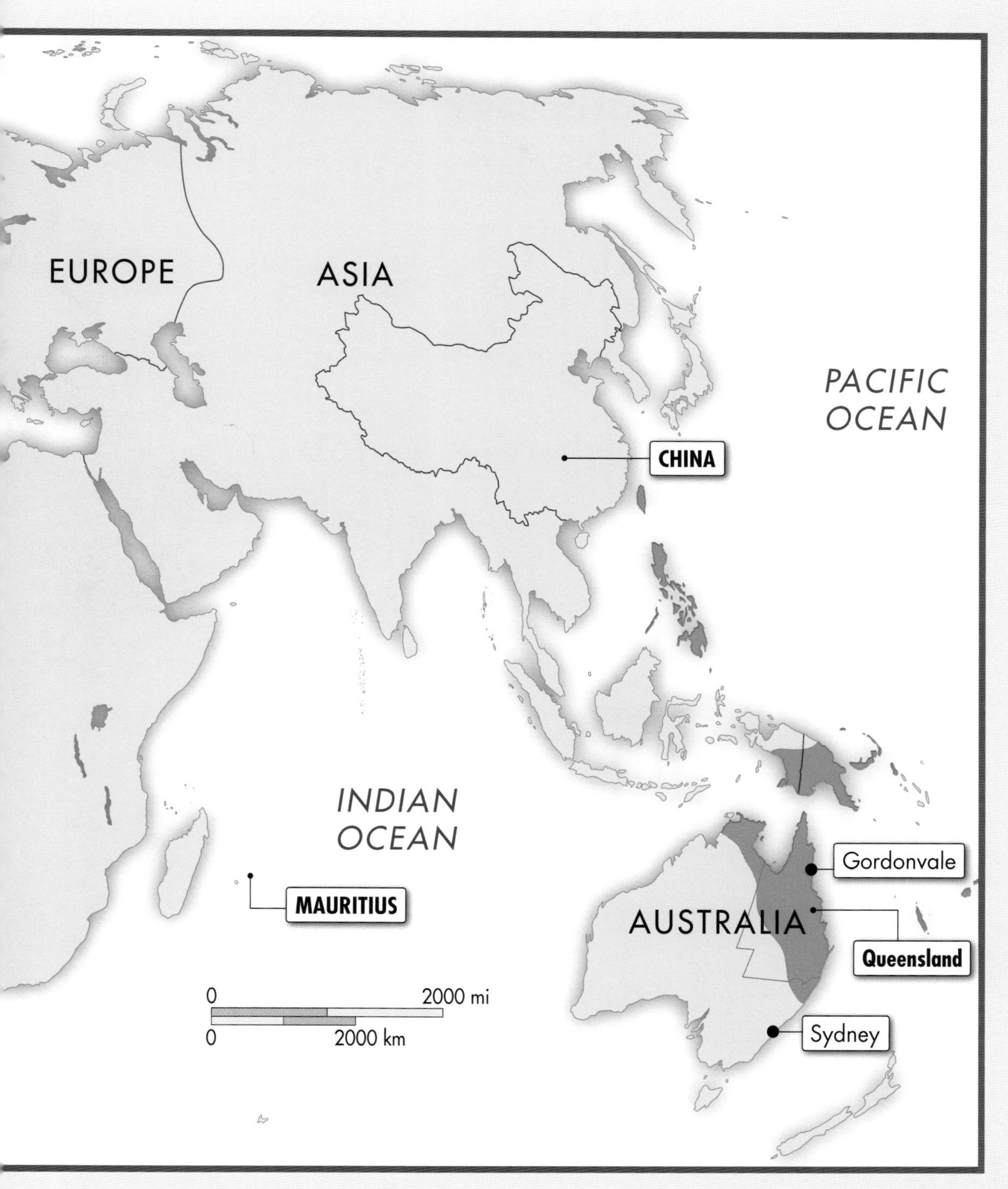

lives naturally and where it has invaded.

GLOSSARY

amphibians (am-FIB-ee-uhnz) cold-blooded animals that spend some time on land but breed and develop to adulthood in water; frogs, toads, and salamanders are amphibians

biological (bye-uh-LOJ-ik-ul) having to do with living beings

fertilize (FUR-tuh-lize) to cause a female egg to produce offspring by joining male sperm with it

juveniles (JOO-vuh-nylz) the young of a species before they reach full adulthood or are able to reproduce

larvae (LAR-vee) the eggs of an insect

parasite (PA-ruh-SITE) a living animal or plant that survives by feeding off, or living on or in, a host plant or animal

parotid gland (pa-ROT-id GLAND) one of two parts of the body below and in front of each ear that in cane toads produces toxin

reptiles (REP-tiles) cold-blooded animals covered with scales or horny plates that breathe with lungs; snakes, turtles, and crocodiles are reptiles

species (SPEE-sheez) a group of similar plants or animals

toxins (TOK-sins) poisons

venom (VEN-uhm) poison produced by some snakes, spiders, toads, and other animals

veterinarian (vet-uhr-uh-NAIR-ee-un) a doctor who specializes in caring for animals

For More Information

Books

Clarke, Barry. *Amphibian.* New York: DK Publishing, 2005.

Gerstein, Sherry, ed. *Animal Planet: The Most Extreme Animals.* San Francisco: Jossey-Bass, 2007.

May, Suellen. *Invasive Aquatic and Wetland Animals.* New York: Chelsea House, 2007.

Web Sites

Cane Toad
honoluluzoo.org/cane_toad.htm
To learn more about the large cane toad at this site run by the Honolulu Zoo

Department of Conservation and Land Management
www.canetoadbattle.com
To download an informational brochure about the cane toad, and discover ways to stop the cane toad invasion in Western Australia

ToadBuster: Protecting Biodiversity
www.frogwatch.org.au/
To read the latest frog news in northern Australia, and get answers to frequently asked questions about cane toads

Index

About the Author

Barbara A. Somervill writes children's nonfiction books on a variety of topics. She is particularly interested in nature and foreign countries. Somervill believes that researching new and different topics makes writing every book an adventure. When she is not writing, Somervill is an avid reader and plays bridge.